What Readers Are Saying About

Every Heart Restored

by Stephen Arterburn and Fred and Brenda Stoeker

"Fred and Brenda Stoeker deal with the sensitive subject of how couples cope in the wake of sexual sin with wisdom and compassion. Their message offers hope to struggling husbands and wives who desire to rebuild their relationships and have Christ-centered marriages free from sexual impurity."

—JILL PHILLIPS, singer-songwriter and recording artist

"The Every Man series has shed light into the hearts of men and on the temptation and trappings of sexual sin. Now *Every Heart Restored* gives women compassionate spiritual insight into the often misunderstood, confusing, and heart-wrenching area of sexual sin."

—DR. GARY AND BARBARA ROSBERG, America's Family Coaches
and authors of *Divorce-Proof Your Marriage*

"Finally, hope has arrived! On behalf of the hundreds of thousands of women whose dreams and hearts are shattered, I say 'Thank you!' The authors of *Every Heart Restored* give women the permission and the authority to confront and put an end to enabling their husband's inappropriate sexual behavior… and tell us that with hard work, accountability, and a constant guarding of the eyes and mind, a man can retrain his brain and keep lust out of one's being and marriage."

—MARSHA MEANS, counselor and author of *Living with Your
Husband's Secret Wars*

"From the very beginning in the garden to the very consummation of all things, it has always been about two with one heart. *Every Heart Restored* is destined to bring deep and intimate healing to the union of hurting husbands and wives desperate to move from the wounds back to the wonder."

—LISA BEVERE, author of *Kissed the Girls and Made Them Cry*

Stephen Arterburn
Fred & Brenda Stoeker with Mike Yorkey

every heart restored

A Wife's Guide to Healing
in the Wake of Every Man's Battle

workbook

WATERBROOK
PRESS

EVERY HEART RESTORED WORKBOOK
PUBLISHED BY WATERBROOK PRESS
2375 Telstar Drive, Suite 160
Colorado Springs, Colorado 80920
A division of Random House, Inc.

ISBN 1-57856-785-8

Copyright © 2004 Stephen Arterburn, Brenda Stoeker, Fred Stoeker, and Mike Yorkey

Published in association with the literary agency of Alive Communications, Inc., 7680 Goddard Street, Suite 200, Colorado Springs, CO 80920.

Printed in the United States of America
2004—First Edition

10 9 8 7 6 5 4 3 2 1

contents

questions you may have about this workbook

What will the *Every Heart Restored Workbook* do for me?

Part of the Every Man series, the *Every Heart Restored Workbook* is designed for wives who have been confronted with their husband's sexual sin. In this workbook you will find biblical truth to stand on, compassion to draw from, questions to learn from. As you try to navigate this path, the *Every Heart Restored Workbook* will give you the tools to take your next steps with confidence and hope.

Is this workbook enough, or do I also need the book *Every Heart Restored*?

Included in each weekly study, you'll find a number of excerpts from *Every Heart Restored,* each marked at the beginning and the end by this symbol: 📖. Nevertheless, the most beneficial approach is to also read *Every Heart Restored* as you go through this companion workbook.

The lessons look long. Do I need to work through each one?

This workbook is designed to guide your exploration of all the material, but you may find it best to focus your time and discussion on some sections and questions more than others.

To help your pacing, we've designed the workbook so it can most easily be used in either an eight-week or a twelve-week program.

- *For the eight-week track,* simply follow the basic organization of the eight different weekly lessons.
- *For the twelve-week track,* save the "going deeper" questions from weeks one and two. Do those for week three. Follow the same pattern for weeks three and four, weeks five and six, and weeks seven and eight (you'll find reminder notes within the text).

Above all, keep in mind that the purpose of the workbook is to assist you in specific applications of the biblical truth taught in *Every Heart Restored.* The wide array of questions included in each weekly study is meant to help you approach this practical application from different angles, with personal reflection and self-examination. Allowing adequate time to prayerfully reflect on each question will be much more valuable to you than rushing through the workbook.

How do I bring together a small group to go through this workbook?

You'll get far more out of this workbook if you're able to work through it with a small group of like-minded women. And what do you do if you don't know of a group that's going through the workbook? Start a group of your own!

Because of the sensitive nature of the topic, you may wonder how you can best approach other women. Begin with your circle of friends. Ask if they might have any interest. They will also have friends who might be struggling with the same issue. Begin by word of mouth. Another option is to approach the women's ministry at your church. If they have a group environment, you might be able to open it up there. Once you have a group (even if it's only a few women), begin meeting weekly or biweekly.

You could schedule your meetings over a lunch hour, first thing in the morning, on a weekday evening, or even on Saturday morning. The meeting place can be a room at church, your living room, an office—whatever is most convenient for your group. But do make sure that you choose a place where your discussion won't be overheard by others, so everyone will be comfortable sharing candidly and freely.

This workbook follows a simple, easy-to-use format. First, each woman completes a week's lesson on her own. Then, when you come together that week, you discuss the content, what you have learned, and the questions or information that were particularly meaningful.

It's best if one person in your group is designated as the facilitator. This person is not a lecturer or teacher, but she simply has the responsibility to keep the discussion moving and to ensure that each woman in the group has an opportunity to join in.

At the beginning, remind the women of the simple ground rule that anything shared in the group stays in the group—everything's confidential. This will help the women feel safer about sharing honestly and openly in an environment of trust.

Finally, we encourage you during each meeting to allow time for prayer—conversational, short-sentence prayers expressed honestly before God. He is the author of healing, and as it says in Matthew 18:20, "Where two or three come together in my name, there am I with them."

facing betrayal

Eight-week track—Week One
Twelve-week track—Week One

Dusk had just settled when Andrea walked into his office. The lights were off, and her husband, Dan, was sitting at his computer. He didn't hear her approach. The images on the screen caught Andrea's breath in her throat. *It must be a mistake,* she thought. *He'll shut the computer down as soon as he realizes what popped up.*

But Dan didn't turn off the computer. He didn't turn away. His eyes were glued to the screen as he clicked through to more and more graphic images.

"Dan?"

When he turned, she almost didn't recognize her husband of five years. The immediate embarrassment and ensuing anger poured off of him in quick, painful waves.

She stumbled backward and went to the living room, collapsing onto the couch.

He didn't follow.

Later that night Andrea gathered the courage to confront him. Yes, he viewed pornography. It had been going on since before they were married. He was defensive, angry. It wasn't until the early morning hours that he seemed to soften. Finally, he put his head in his hands. Yes, he said, it was getting worse, and yes, maybe it was becoming a problem.

Andrea felt overwhelmed, betrayed, and heartbroken.

What was she supposed to do now?

📖 EVERY WOMAN'S TRUTH
(Your Personal Journey into God's Word)

As you read Andrea's story, it may sound hauntingly similar to your own. Maybe you didn't stumble across him at the computer, but perhaps he asked you to watch a movie, or you ran across a stash of magazines, or you opened the phone bill to discover too many unfamiliar and costly calls.

Your breath caught in your throat, your heart pounded, and for more than a moment you didn't want to believe it was happening to you.

The emotions you are feeling are very real. You have every right to feel betrayed, to feel angry and demeaned. Loving your husband, believing in your marriage, taking steps toward healing—these things do *not* mean that you bury your emotions, ignore them, or move on without acknowledging them. In fact, you *have* to address them in order to take any steps forward. What he is doing is wrong. He should not be looking at other women in that way. He is hurting you and your marriage, and you may feel overwhelmed with emotion.

Sometimes you may just need permission to feel.

As Brenda shared in *Every Heart Restored:*

> 📖 We have every right to expect normal Christian behavior from our husbands, and when we don't get it, it's normal for us to feel hurt and disappointment. Each Christian wife deserves the same gift that Fred has given me, and no argument can dissuade me from believing that. If your husband

is not leading a disciplined life, he is robbing you, so you naturally feel crushed.

What other feelings will surge over you in the wake of his porn and the masturbation that follows? Anger, for one. When Fred's business office was robbed a few years ago, we were both furious. Why not? It's normal to be angry when you've been robbed, and so it's normal to be angry at your husband's sexual sin. 📖

So what can you do? You need to know that in your moments of anger, you have somewhere to go. You have a refuge and a strength you can lean on. Meditate on these verses and cry out to your heavenly Father. Know that He grieves with you. His ear is one you can trust; His shoulder is one you can lean on. Even if you feel anger toward God Himself, let Him know. His shoulders are big and strong enough, and He is ready and waiting to meet you.

O LORD my God, I take refuge in you;
     save and deliver me. (Psalm 7:1)

The LORD is a refuge for the oppressed,
     a stronghold in times of trouble. (Psalm 9:9)

Turn your ear to me,
     come quickly to my rescue,
be my rock of refuge,
     a strong fortress to save me. (Psalm 31:2)

The LORD is my strength and my song;
     he has become my salvation. (Psalm 118:14)

He gives strength to the weary. (Isaiah 40:29)

As a mother comforts her child,

so will I comfort you. (Isaiah 66:13)

It might be tempting to read these passages and wonder how they could possibly help the hurt you are feeling. But this is about going to the One who knows you best and laying it on the line. Let Him hear your heart—and then lay hold of His promises. He loves you profoundly, and your hurts are His own. Be real with Him; pour out your sense of betrayal, your anger, your grief. He is not a God relegated to church pews and sanctuaries. He is a God intimately and deeply connected to all that you are experiencing. He is about getting in the messes and sustaining you. Call to Him, and He will be there.

1. Sometimes it feels safer not to feel anything at all. We don't want to hurt or be angry or feel the betrayal. So we stuff our emotions. But what would happen to both you and your marriage if you stuffed all of your emotions inside and didn't expose them?

2. Do you believe you can call out to God in real ways and that He will hear you? What do the above scriptures say about God's ability to meet you in your pain?

3. If you were to take the space below and write out your heart to God, what would you tell Him? How can you begin the process of giving Him access to your hurt? (If you begin to write to God, and the words flow, grab a notebook and keep going. Don't let limited space stop you!)

☑ **EVERY WOMAN'S CHOICE**
(Questions for Personal Reflection and Examination)

📖 When your trust is in shambles, there is only one person you can rely on—Jesus Christ. He understands pain all too well, and He's well acquainted with grief. He's here to comfort you and to build an intimate relationship with you, the only one that lasts for eternity. 📖

📖 These feelings are plain awful, and you know you will have to do something about them if you're ever to begin rebuilding your life with him. But what do you do with them? You may be wishing you could just forget the mess and let these feelings go, passing them off as overreactions. So would he.

But even if you *could* manage that, something tells you that this would be the worst thing you could possibly do. 📖

4. What are you feeling right now? (List the emotions that come to mind.)

5. If you could identify one emotion that most consumes you, what would it be? (Betrayal? Embarrassment? Humiliation? Shame? Anger? Sadness?) Describe the feeling and why it is so prominent.

6. If your child had just experienced a crushing hurt, wouldn't your heart be heavy for her? How might God be feeling about what you have just written in answer to the above questions?

Close your eyes. Take a minute to feel God's tenderness toward you. Let Him comfort your heart. Jot down what you hear from him.

⟡ EVERY WOMAN'S WALK
(Your Guide to Personal Application)

As you explore your emotions, you may feel guilty for feeling some of them. *How long will this take?* you may think. *When will I get over this?* You may be tempted to rush through, because anger can feel so "unspiritual." You may be frustrated by your own sadness or surprised that it pops up on a regular basis.

Yes, God does call us to work through our anger and forgive. He does ask us to move forward and not to get stuck in bitterness. And He reminds us not to sin in our anger. That's all true. But often we want to skip right from the hurt we have received to the forgiveness. We may scold ourselves for experiencing pain long after the incident. Or conversely, we may hold on to our anger fiercely, afraid to let it go.

The best way to approach this is to continually bring your heart to God. You will need Him, because all you are feeling may seem to be getting worse before it gets better. This is a journey, with all the hills and valleys that accompany a hard path. But your Father is with you. Come to Him and pour it out. When you are at His feet, He'll guide you through the messy feelings. And remember, it's hard to remain bitter when you are embraced in a love beyond compare. It is hard to close your heart and stay stuck when you're spending time with the true and living God. He'll direct your heart. Just stay close.

So what can you do? How can you experience anger in righteous ways, moving toward forgiveness and healing in your marriage?

It's a process. And here are some tools that may help along the way:

- *Feel the emotion.* Allow yourself the time and the privacy to expose your heart to yourself and to God.
- *Hold on to the truth.* Let God be your refuge and your strength. Plaster verses of comfort and hope where you can see them

often. Remind yourself of His ability to be and provide all that you need.

- *Talk to someone.* Often God will use another believer, a female friend, a pastor, or a professional Christian counselor to act as His hands and feet. You need to know that you are not alone and that others will stand with you. If you don't have someone you can talk to, keep your eyes open for solid believers at your church and begin to build relationships with them.

- *Understand that it takes time.* Grant yourself grace. After the initial incident, it takes time to heal. In fact, the wound may be reopened as your husband continues to struggle. Understand that your healing is not a one-day occurrence. It takes time in the presence of the only One who can heal. Cling to Him and remember Zechariah 1:17 where the Lord promises to *again* comfort Zion. His comfort isn't a one-time deal. He is always ready and willing.

7. Where are you in the process of feeling what is in your heart?

8. What practical steps can you take to deal with your emotions, to take them to your heavenly Father? Can you journal your thoughts to Him? Get on your knees? Go off into the woods? Close your door and curl up around your pillow? Can you arrange time with your Strength and Refuge today?

9. Do you have someone you can talk to? If not, what are some steps you can take to begin building that relationship or to seek counseling?

10. Do you have a time frame on how long you are "allowed" to be angry? What do you think your recovery process should be? How do you think God feels about this process?

👥 EVERY WOMAN'S TALK
(Going Deeper—Constructive Topics and Questions for Group Discussion)

(For the twelve-week track, save these questions for week three.)

> 📖 Like the heart-wrenching scene from *Gone with the Wind,* you naively trust that everything will work out somehow, passionately muttering like Scarlett O'Hara, "I can't think about this today.... I'll go crazy if I do. I'll think about it tomorrow." 📖

> 📖 "I was getting further and further away from God during the years leading up to my husband's disclosure of his sexual sin. I was so caught up in looking at my husband and trying

to figure out what was wrong with him—trying to pull him back to where we once were. My focus was entirely upon my husband and my family, but that's because our marriage was in trouble. After finding out about the sin, I realized that this was bigger than me. I needed God's help." 📖

A. Through this chapter, what has God communicated about the emotions He has given you?

B. Do you agree that working through your anger can set you up to begin healing? Why or why not?

C. Do you believe that God can draw you close in this process? Are you willing to let Him? Why or why not?

D. What is one step you can take toward your healing? Share it with the group and ask for their accountability and prayer.

fighting the shame

Eight-week track—Week Two

Twelve-week track—Week Two

"It's not like any other marriage problem," Terri said to the group. "It's not about money or whether he picks up his socks. It's about sexuality. It's about the most intimate aspect of our relationship." She paused, "I can tell someone that my husband has slipped up and gone on a spending spree. I can't tell them that he slipped up and looked at pornography. People look at me differently. I look at me differently. I feel so embarrassed, like there must be something wrong with me that he has to go outside of our relationship to find stimulation. I hate it. It's humiliating."

EVERY WOMAN'S TRUTH
(Your Personal Journey into God's Word)

Battling shame is a natural part of the healing process. You feel embarrassed by his addiction and rejected by the intimate nature of it. It's very difficult not to carry the weight of that humiliation on your own shoulders. You may be afraid to tell anyone what you are experiencing. You may feel like Terri, that there is something wrong with you—and the last thing you want is for other people to know. So you hide from your husband, you hide from others, you hide from yourself. It feels too painful to do anything else.

Here is the truth: you do not have to be ashamed! What has happened in your marriage is tragic, but it is not insurmountable and it is not uncommon. Many wives deal with some form of this struggle simply because of our culture and the nature of male sexuality. We'll talk about that more when we get to chapters 4 and 5, but for now, please begin to wrap yourself around the truth—this addiction is *not about you.*

As you take your shame and your embarrassment to your heavenly Father, as you expose it to His light, He can begin to comfort you with His truth.

> You are my lamp, O LORD;
> > the Lord turns my darkness into light. (2 Samuel 22:29)

> In you I trust, O my God.
> Do not let me be put to shame,
> > nor let my enemies triumph over me. (Psalm 25:2)

> Those who look to him are radiant;
> > their faces are never covered with shame. (Psalm 34:5)

> The LORD is close to the brokenhearted
> > and saves those who are crushed in spirit. (Psalm 34:18)

> Along unfamiliar paths I will guide them;
> I will turn the darkness into light before them
> > and make the rough places smooth.
> These are the things I will do;
> > I will not forsake them. (Isaiah 42:16)

> As the Scripture says, "Anyone who trusts in him will never
> be put to shame." (Romans 10:11)

God lights the dark places. He turns shame and darkness into hope and light. It's part of who He is and what He does. The enemy would love to drown out any hope of healing in your life. He would like to keep you stuck in humiliation, afraid even to go to your Father in heaven. He would like to turn your husband's sin into a painful secret that you keep—taking away your joy and your hope.

But in God's hands, in His light, healing can begin.

1. You need never be ashamed in God's presence. He is the first place you can go with any sense of humiliation. As you meditate on the scriptures listed previously, what do you discover about God's character and what He can do with those dark, secret places?

2. Romans 10:11 says that anyone who trusts in God will never be put to shame. How does that apply to your situation?

3. As you grow in trusting God, in experiencing His love for you, and in believing that love to your core, shame will have no place in your heart. Do you believe God's love for you? The value He has placed on you? If you struggle with that, write a prayer to Him in the space below. Ask Him for help.

☑ EVERY WOMAN'S CHOICE
(Questions for Personal Reflection and Examination)

📖 Don't be too hard on yourself. Patrick Middleton, who counsels those bound up in sexual addiction, told us, "It is not uncommon for wives to know for some time that something is wrong with their sexual relationship, but they dismiss their feelings of disconnection and shame as being crazy. For some reason, they refuse to trust their own intuition, which is plainly telling them something is wrong." 📖

📖 On your darker days you now even suspect that he conveniently led you to believe that you were to blame, intentionally and artfully using your guilt, fear, and disciplined regimens to cover the tracks of his undisciplined life. How stupid you feel! How conned! 📖

4. Maybe you wrote out a prayer in response to question 3, asking God for help in feeling His love. One way to experience the type of love that chases away shame is to talk with someone who will not judge you. Would you be willing to share your story with someone? Why or why not?

5. If you could talk about your insecurities and receive love and encouragement in return, how do you think your heart would respond? How would that move you toward healing?

6. Sometimes we unintentionally choose someone who is not safe to share our hearts with. We might get hurt or discouraged by her response. Should we give up trying? Why or why not?

Opening up about your situation will give you a support network outside of your home. Whether that person is a pastor, a friend, a counselor, or a small group, you need to be reminded that your husband's sin does not have to remain a source of shame for you. And while your embarrassment is justified, truth wrapped in love can take the sting from it.

Allow God to remove your shame by calling out to Him. Allow Him to reach you through the helping hands of other believers.

ᕦ EVERY WOMAN'S WALK
(Your Guide to Personal Application)

As you consider opening your heart to God and to others, you may feel overwhelmed with emotion. Sometimes when we speak about pain in our lives, it seems too real, too overwhelming, too much to bear. We think that if we tuck it away, keep it a "private" matter, that we will be honoring our husband and ourselves.

While there is definitely room for discretion (no announcements in the church bulletin), it's the secrets and the hiding that offer a breeding ground for shame.

This concept of sharing, of pouring our hearts out to God and others, is not just a good idea; it's a biblical concept. David and Jonathan were close friends. Their story is told in 1 Samuel. As friends they celebrated each other's victories and fought each other's battles. Jonathan's father wanted to kill David—talk about the potential for shame! But Jonathan stood fast beside his friend, and David stood fast beside Jonathan. They were able to remind each other of the truth, of their love, and because of that, shame had no place.

We may not have an individual in our lives that represents a David or a Jonathan. But as believers, we are to take on each other's battles and celebrate each other's victories. You are in a battle right now. You need other believers.

7. Forecasting ahead, what would it do for your marriage if you had someone alongside you, praying for you, lifting you up, encouraging you?

8. If you haven't already, it's time to take a step toward another believer. Can you think of someone you can approach? If so, write her name and a plan of action for how and when you will connect with her.

9. Are you willing to commit to seeking help? Write down a statement of commitment to yourself, a promise to move forward in this area.

🙂🙂 EVERY WOMAN'S TALK

(Going Deeper—Constructive Topics and Questions for Group Discussion)

(For the twelve-week track, save these questions for week three.)

> 📖 We definitely urge you to be purposeful about surrounding yourself with godly sisters who are navigating the same

waters, because confiding in them can make all the differ-
ence in the world. You don't want to blab your husband's
problems all over town, but being able to vent and pray
with someone who cares for you can do wonders for your
sanity. 📖

📖 Women are relationally driven, and they need to share
their stories with one another for the emotional support that
brings, but they also need the wise instruction from those
who've traveled these seas before them. 📖

But those who hope in the LORD
    will renew their strength. (Isaiah 40:31)

Some men came carrying a paralytic on a mat and tried to
take him into the house to lay him before Jesus. When they
could not find a way to do this because of the crowd, they
went up on the roof and lowered him on his mat through
the tiles into the middle of the crowd, right in front of Jesus.
(Luke 5:18-19)

Carry each other's burdens, and in this way you fulfill the
law of Christ. (Galatians 6:2)

A. Through this chapter and God's Word, what have you learned regarding shame?

B. When you bring your shame to God's feet, He is able to light the dark places. What is your plan of action for exposing your heart to Him?

C. As you read about the friends in Luke 5 who carried the paralytic and lowered him to the feet of Jesus, what do you understand about the value of friendship in healing?

D. How does the support and encouragement of others diminish shame?

E. If you understand that you are not alone in your struggles, and you realize the benefits of having community and help, think about this: is there anything else that keeps you from exposing your story? If so, what is it? And what can you do to apply truth in that area?

F. What is one step you can take in broadening your support base? Share it with the group and ask for their accountability and prayer.

discovering your beauty

For the twelve-week track, complete discussion questions for weeks one and two this week.

Eight-week track—Week Three

Twelve-week track—Week Four

Jenna stepped from the shower and quickly wrapped a towel around her body. She didn't even glance in the mirror until she was fully covered. She hated her reflection. After discovering her husband's addiction to pornography, the sight of her own body left her even more depressed and heartbroken.

There was no way she could compare with the airbrushed figures in his magazines. No way her extended arms would be as inviting as the seductive poses of the women he encountered on the Internet.

While her husband was trying to give up pornography, she knew that he often struggled. Knowing that he entertained other images in his head made Jenna feel less desirable with each passing day.

Yet just yesterday Jenna's best friend told her how beautiful she was. She'd insisted on it. Brushing back her hair from her forehead, she'd reminded Jenna of both her inner and outer beauty.

Beautiful? Jenna scoffed to herself as she caught a glimpse in the mirror, *not even close.*

📖 EVERY WOMAN'S TRUTH
(Your Personal Journey into God's Word)

One of the most painful wounds inflicted through pornography is how terrible a woman can feel about her own beauty. Someone else has captured her man's eye. When the intimate exposure of her vulnerable nudity is rejected for another, it is the ultimate slap in the face.

As a thinking individual, you can be told that his sexual addiction has little to do with you. And with time and understanding, you can even begin to believe it. As we'll discuss in chapters 4 and 5, it *is* about old wounds, male wiring, and societal brokenness. Yes, you can know all that in your head—but when it comes to your heart, that's something else entirely.

As you work through the betrayal and the shame of your husband's sin, there is something else you need to understand. You are *beautiful.* You are a handcrafted treasure in the eyes of your God. He loves first and foremost your inner beauty. He is captivated by the ways you have sacrificed for your family. He finds you breathtaking as you cook yet another meal, as you bandage a scrape, nurture a friend, or take care of a sick husband or child. Even when you are frustrated and not at your best, He delights in how you compose yourself, smile ruefully, and try to honor His ways.

Physically, He loves the way your smile reaches up to your eyes, the way you laugh out loud when something strikes you as funny. He adores the curve of your face, the way you dress up, and the way you dress down by donning your favorite pair of old jeans. He chuckles with pleasure when you wake up with "bed head," and He can't get enough of the beauty you expose when you are feeling playful.

You are His delight. Read for yourself:

The king is enthralled by your beauty. (Psalm 45:11)

For you created my inmost being;
   you knit me together in my mother's womb.
I praise you because I am fearfully and wonderfully made;
   your works are wonderful,
   I know that full well.
My frame was not hidden from you
   when I was made in the secret place.
When I was woven together in the depths of the earth,
   your eyes saw my unformed body. (Psalm 139:13-16)

He has made everything beautiful in its time.
(Ecclesiastes 3:11)

How beautiful you are, my darling!
   Oh, how beautiful!
   Your eyes are doves! (Song of Songs 1:15)

...to bestow on them a crown of beauty
   instead of ashes,
the oil of gladness
   instead of mourning. (Isaiah 61:3)

For we are God's workmanship, created in Christ Jesus.
(Ephesians 2:10)

Not only does God find you captivating, He is also able to take the
hurt you are experiencing now—the "ashes" of your dreams—and turn
them into something beautiful as well.

He is good, and He is absolutely crazy about you. Hold on to that, cling to His truth. Especially when you feel overwhelmed by the voices and feelings that try to whisper something different.

You may think, *Well, it's great that God thinks I'm beautiful, but I want my husband to find me attractive!* That makes total sense, so of course you do! But know this, if you believe what God says about you, your sense of personal beauty won't be tied up in your husband's actions; it will be founded on the truth. That in itself will give you freedom to smile, freedom to be confident, and freedom to walk through this situation with your head held high.

1. How do you view yourself these days? How has your husband's sin affected your perception of your own beauty?

2. When you reflect on the words of the previously quoted scriptures, can you see and begin to believe how precious you are in God's eyes? Why or why not?

3. For a moment, close your eyes and imagine God's delight in who you are. His eyes light up when He sees you. His mouth breaks into a broad smile. If you can't capture that image, write out your heart to God. Ask Him to show you how He sees you. Call out to Him, and He will help you.

☑ **EVERY WOMAN'S CHOICE**
(Questions for Personal Reflection and Examination)

> 📖 You *have* to know it's not about your attractiveness or sexiness. It's that simple, and that's why I have spent so much time describing male sexuality. The tendrils of sexual sin that choke our lives aren't just sexual and aren't just physical—they reach throughout our being—body, soul, and spirit.
>
> They're about addictions and old habits. They're about wounds and emotional dependence and ignorance and warped wiring. They're about sin—his sin. Your husband is at the root of it, not you. 📖

> 📖 Fred claims that although I can never look like I'm twenty again, his passion for my body *can* remain the same. The Bible says so, and he's taken the following scripture to heart: "Let your fountain [of human life] be blessed [with the rewards of fidelity], and rejoice in the wife of your youth. Let her be as the loving hind and pleasant doe [tender,

gentle, attractive]—let her bosom satisfy you at all times, and always be transported with delight in her love. Why should you, my son, be infatuated with a loose woman, embrace the bosom *(physically or visually)* of an outsider, and go astray?

"For the ways of man are directly before the eyes of the Lord, and He [Who would have us live soberly, chastely, and godly] carefully weighs all man's goings.

"His own iniquities shall ensnare the wicked man, and he shall be held with the cords of his sin. He will die for lack of discipline and instruction, and in the greatness of his folly he will go astray and be lost" (Proverbs 5:18-23, AMP).

Obviously, it *is* possible for a man to take joy in the wife of his youth and to be always and only ravished by her beauty alone…*if* he exhibits the discipline to do so. 📖

When your marriage works according to God's design, your beauty remains captivating through a lifetime of living and loving together. That means that God has made you beautiful! Because your husband is looking elsewhere, it does not mean that you are not beautiful—it means that he has stepped outside of God's plan.

4. Can you begin to separate your husband's sin from your perception of yourself? Why or why not?

5. In the picture God creates of marriage, your beauty is meant to captivate your husband for a lifetime. As you reflect on the past, that may bring grief and sadness to your heart. Yet it can also bring you hope for the future. How can God's plan for marriage offer you hope today?

6. How could believing in your own beauty (as a handcrafted treasure of God) positively affect your marriage?

⤳ EVERY WOMAN'S WALK
(Your Guide to Personal Application)

It seems easy to *say* that your beauty isn't influenced by your husband's choices. But how can you really take that truth as your own? What does it look like?

God's truth is not always something we read once and immediately apply. If we have believed a lie for years, it takes time and effort to let the truth settle into our hearts. But this *is* the truth. You are a beautiful woman, a handcrafted treasure. It doesn't matter if you are old, young, heavy, thin, short, or tall. God doesn't look at people the way we look at people. Hollywood will tell you that beauty is defined in very specific, narrow ways. God says something entirely different. First Samuel 16:7 says, "But the LORD said to Samuel, 'Do not consider his appearance or his height, for I have rejected him. The LORD does not look at the things man looks at. Man looks at the outward appearance, but the LORD looks at the heart."

So what can you do? How can you begin to accept this truth? By realizing that it *does* matter. As you have a greater understanding of your own value and beauty outside of your husband's sin, you will be able to extend compassion and grace when the time calls for it. You will be able to cast aside shame and work through your anger. You will reside firmly in the hand of your God, basking in His love and passion for you. Understanding this truth is incredibly important and will pave the way for healing and restoration.

7. Where are you in the process of believing in your own beauty?

8. Can you understand the importance of seeing yourself through God's eyes? Why does it matter? (Use your own words.)

9. If you have lived with a broken image of your own beauty for a long time, it will take some hard work to change the old messages in your head. What scriptures (presented in this chapter) can help you? Write them down in the space below and then write them someplace where you can see them daily.

10. Take a moment and write down traits that are beautiful in you. If you can't think of any, ask God for His help. He has a whole list!

◑◐ EVERY WOMAN'S TALK
(Going Deeper—Constructive Topics and Questions for Group Discussion)

(For the twelve-week track, save these questions for week six.)

> 📖 If you've ignored such clues, you feel like a fool, another common emotion swamping wives in the wake [of betrayal]. But that feeling becomes an overwhelming flood if you've beat yourself up over his lack of sexual desire over the past few years, figuring that your "home cooking" should have kept him coming back for more if it tasted any good.
>
> Out of guilt you may have shouldered the whole load of responsibility for his lack of desire—maybe dieting hard to

lose weight and pouring out sweat in heavy workouts to draw out the desires of your one and only. Perhaps you've stopped by Victoria's Secret in order to drape yourself in something visually tantalizing to spark his attentions, even though wearing it made you feel uncomfortable. And often, when you bravely initiated a passionate encounter, your vulnerability was flung back in your face. 📖

📖 It *is* possible for a man to take joy in the wife of his youth and to be always and only ravished by her beauty alone…*if* he exhibits the discipline to do so. What's more, since it's God's Word that defines what normal behavior is for Christians, we're also forced to conclude that the discipline of guarding the eyes and the heart is not only possible but that God considers such discipline to be normal among His sons. 📖

A. Have you blamed yourself for your husband's lack of physical desire, doing what you can to entice him, only to find rejection? How have you interpreted that?

B. Is his behavior about your beauty or supposed lack thereof? Why or why not?

C. What is the truth concerning your value—according to God's Word?

D. As you look at the other women in your group, can you see what is beautiful and captivating about them? Take a moment to share with one another the beauty you see.

E. If you could take one practical step toward rebuilding your own perspective of your beauty, what would it be? Share it with your group and ask for prayer and accountability.

understanding
his addiction I

Eight-week track—Week Four

Twelve-week track—Week Five

John was only twelve when he stumbled across a stash of pornographic magazines in his father's office. Electrified by the images he saw there, he returned as often as possible to get another glimpse. As he showered each morning, he would call up those images and masturbate. He felt guilty, and each time he promised himself he would never do it again.

Years later John had branched out into Internet pornography and magazines of his own. Just like his father before him, he kept his addiction hidden and suffered silently with his shame. At the same time, John was growing as a young believer. He wanted to please God, but it seemed like he had little control over his mind.

When John met Sara, he thought he would be able to put pornography behind him. She was a beautiful Christian girl who truly loved him. He believed that once he married, he could express his sexuality in healthy ways, and the longing for pornography would diminish.

It didn't.

Now he'd been exposed. Sara, as innocent and loving as he could have ever hoped for, had stumbled across his stash. She was heartbroken, and he was ashamed. Would she ever be able to understand how helpless he felt?

📖 EVERY WOMAN'S TRUTH
(Your Personal Journey into God's Word)

The reasons and motives behind sexual addiction run as far and wide as the reasons for drug use, obesity, or even sexual promiscuity. It's a sin that can be traced back to any number of diverse factors in a man's life.

So, you may say, *who cares? He hurt me! Why should I go through the trouble of understanding him?* Because you need to know that his choice was not about betraying you; it was about so much more that had to do with *him.* Understanding this will give you the courage and the desire to help him.

As we discuss some of the reasons that a man may get stuck in this trap, you'll need to set aside your hurt for a moment. That's why we walked through the truth of your betrayal, the importance of dealing with shame, and the value of finding your beauty in the statements of your Creator. Once you have some of those things settled, you will see beyond the heartache and begin to offer compassion to a man who is stuck, helpless and lost in something that may feel too big to conquer.

Why? Why should you have to? Because God calls us to love, to forgive, and to have compassion on others. Why? Because we desperately need it ourselves.

Read on:

> For all have sinned and fall short of the glory of God.
> (Romans 3:23)

Therefore, the kingdom of heaven is like a king who wanted to settle accounts with his servants. As he began the settlement, a man who owed him ten thousand talents was brought to him. Since he was not able to pay, the master ordered that he and his wife and his children and all that he had be sold to repay the debt.

The servant fell on his knees before him. "Be patient with me," he begged, "and I will pay back everything." The servant's master took pity on him, cancelled the debt and let him go.

But when that servant went out, he found one of his fellow servants who owed him a hundred denarii. He grabbed him and began to choke him. "Pay back what you owe me!" he demanded.

His fellow servant fell to his knees and begged him, "Be patient with me, and I will pay you back."

But he refused. Instead, he went off and had the man thrown into prison until he could pay the debt. (Matthew 18:23-30)

First, according to Romans 3:23, we have all sinned. We are all broken, imperfect people who often run to sin when we are hurting, scared, angry, or full of pride. You do the same. This truth isn't meant to take away from the pain you are experiencing, but it is meant to help you see that there is "not one" who gets it right all the time. If, in humility, you can see where you have made poor choices, you may better be able to understand how your husband was trapped and what you can do to love him through the struggle.

Second, God offered us extravagant grace. How can we not do the same? The servant in Matthew 18 had a tremendous debt to pay, only to have it completely wiped clean. But then he had the audacity to call in a much smaller debt from a fellow servant.

Does that mean that we don't hold our husbands accountable? No, and we'll discuss more on that in chapter 6. But it does mean that we tread carefully, remembering always that we, too, are simply recipients of a grace we don't deserve, a love we can't understand, and a forgiveness we can never presume to repay.

In this scenario, grace may take the form of understanding. As you begin to grapple with what brought this into your husband's life, you will be in a better position to extend to him the grace he needs, the grace that might ultimately help open the door to healing.

1. As you meditate on the previously quoted scriptures, what do you think God is asking you to do?

2. Take a moment and think about something in your own life for which you have needed God's extravagant grace. Jot a note of gratitude to your heavenly Father for loving you through that struggle and ask Him to help you do the same with your husband.

☑ EVERY WOMAN'S CHOICE
(Questions for Personal Reflection and Examination)

As mentioned earlier, several factors can contribute to sexual addiction. Each of these contributing factors (and more) is discussed in the book *Every Heart Restored.* In this chapter we'll cover the nature of male sexuality, and we'll discuss a few more factors in chapter 5:

> 📖 We come hardwired with certain qualities that make it very tough to remain sexually pure. We don't need a date or a mistress—our male eyes give us the ability to sin just about any time we want. All we need is a long, lingering look at a partially clothed or unclothed female body to receive a jolt of sexual pleasure.
>
> We aren't picky, either. The jolt can come just as easily from staring at the tight sweater on the girl on the bus to work as it can from a romantic interlude with our wife. In short, we have a visual ignition switch when it comes to the female anatomy, and it takes very little to flip it on.
>
> Women seldom understand this, because they aren't naturally stimulated in the same way. Think back to your high-school days. Did you get turned on when the guys' swim team paraded around in their skimpy bright blue Speedos—the ones with the telltale bulge? The answer is likely a resounding no! In fact, if you're anything like Brenda, you were probably grossed out. Why? The ignition switch for women is tied to touch and relationship—not to the guy's body. It's just the opposite for us as guys. Our eyes hug all the curves, and given the fact that it's pretty easy to see a lot of skin and tight tops in America these days, it's no

surprise that there's a natural desire to take a good look. It's no wonder that men's eyes resist control without conscious effort....

For guys, impurity of the eyes is a type of sexual foreplay. That's right. It can create the same sexual buildup as stroking an inner thigh or rubbing a breast....

Without conscious discipline, our visual foreplay is rarely confined to the marriage bed, and that's when it becomes detestable....

[This] makes it easier to understand why so many otherwise godly men fall into sexual sin. With abundant sensual images so close at hand, men naturally and easily engage in this visual foreplay and fall to sexual temptation—simply by being male. 📖

3. Can you see the value in understanding where your husband's addiction has come from? Are you willing to understand how he is wired as a man, what wounds lie in his past, what might be below the symptoms of his addiction? Why or why not?

4. If a man is hardwired to be visual, how might that add to his struggle—especially in the culture in which we live?

5. Obviously you have noticed that your husband is hardwired to be visual if he is struggling with pornographic images. How does it make you feel to know that as far as his wiring is concerned, he is "normal"?

6. If your husband is unwilling to do anything about his current addiction, does understanding his wiring help you? Why or why not?

⁓ EVERY WOMAN'S WALK
(Your Guide to Personal Application)

📖 *But my husband is a Christian! Why can't he simply pray about this and stop it?* We can go to the altar of prayer and be freed, but if we stop short and never fully close the gates of our eyes to sensual pollution, the sewage seeps right back in, day in and day out. When the chemical highs return, we're captured again. 📖

📖 Probably the most surprising and most valuable thing I've learned about a husband's sexual impurity is that it works more like a habit than a choice. Before Fred helped me understand this, I just assumed that men always chose what they looked at. I didn't know that their eyes are naturally drawn toward anything sensual around them.

More than anything else, this has helped me understand why sexual sin is such a difficult sin to break. I used to think, *If a guy loves his wife enough, he'll simply stop.* Clearly, it's not that simple. Unless they train their eyes and minds, men will be naturally prone to consume everything sensual that comes their way.... This helps me have mercy on men regarding the false starts they make in their effort to win their personal battles. 📖

7. Can you see that understanding your husband may help you to celebrate his smaller victories and comprehend his failures? Explain.

8. Think what it might be like if you were struggling with overeating, smoking, or any other kind of compulsive behavior. What if your husband sat down with you and expressed love and understanding (instead of condemnation), even if the behavior was hurting him personally? How might his compassion affect you?

9. If your husband is sincerely sorry and is trying to work through his addiction, what do you think it would mean to *him* if you sat with him and expressed understanding for where he is struggling? What can you do to communicate that understanding? And if you don't understand it, what can you do to expand your knowledge in this area?

10. Knowing how he is designed, what are some other practical things you can do to help him in this battle?

👥 EVERY WOMAN'S TALK

(Going Deeper—Constructive Topics and Questions for Group Discussion)

(For the twelve-week track, save these questions for week six.)

> 📖 This is another reason why pornography habits are so tough to break: men receive a natural chemical high from looking at pictures of nude women. When our eyes lock onto images of nude women, pleasure chemicals bathe the limbic pleasure centers in the brain, and because it feels good, we want to come back for another hit (look). Quite often then, our addictive behaviors are not rooted in some

lack of love for our wives. Rather, they're linked to the pleasure highs triggered by the images entering the eyes. 📖

A. Is it possible for you to separate your husband's struggle with pornography or lust from his love for you? What can help this process?

B. If a man were to berate our need for relational connection and communication, we would find that insensitive and cruel. How might understanding your husband's visual stimulation benefit his heart and your marriage?

C. Extending grace and having compassion on your husband does not mean that you ignore blatant sin and continued resistance to truth. How can you discern what your husband needs at this point? Share your situation with the group and ask for their feedback.

D. One of the most difficult things in the world is to turn and offer compassion after you have been hurt. If appropriate, think of one thing you can do to extend compassion to your husband and then ask the group for prayer and accountability.

understanding
his addiction II

For the twelve-week track, complete discussion questions for weeks four and five this week.

Eight-week track—Week Five

Twelve-week track—Week Seven

Daniel heard it from all fronts. His father constantly reminded him of all his failures, his classmates demeaned him, and his brother managed to beat him in every game or competition. When Daniel stumbled across pornography at the age of eleven, he discovered a place where he felt strong and unbeatable. The women on the pages of the magazine were posing just for him—nothing was denied him, and he thrived on the sense of excitement and power. Soon he began masturbating to the images, and in those moments the pleasure far outweighed the pain of his experiences.

Daniel also attended a youth group. One of his best friends brought some other magazines for Daniel, and they looked them over closely as they huddled in the church basement. Nothing was ever said about pornography at youth group. Nothing was ever said at church. Nothing was ever said at home.

His habit continued to grow. Even after a successful career and a marriage to a beautiful woman, Daniel still felt most powerful and complete in the presence of the naked women posing "just for him."

☑ EVERY WOMAN'S CHOICE
(Questions for Personal Reflection and Examination)

When Daniel married Wendy, she had no idea what wounds lingered in his heart. *And* she had no idea that he had found a medicine of choice—pornography and masturbation. Wendy couldn't know how Daniel's dad failed him, how his classmates had denied him friendship, how the church had failed to equip him for purity. Wendy was simply stuck with the result of Daniel's sin, and she was feeling horrible about her own identity as a wife—even though she had inflicted none of Daniel's wounds.

Most men have been ill equipped to deal with the visual stimulation that surrounds them. They've been let down by their families and by the churches meant to prepare them. Does this truth take away from a man's responsibility? Not at all. But it may help you, as his wife, to again understand that this issue has more to do with his story than it ever had to do with you.

> 📖 Manhood is a confusing, foggy maze, even for men.
> Consider this: even though I was valedictorian and athlete
> of the year in high school, and even though I'd graduated with
> honors from Stanford University and beaten Dad head-to-
> head in career sales while working in separate territories for
> the same company, my father never accepted me as a real

man. And for many of those years, I wasn't so sure he was
wrong. 📖

📖 Wounds like this—that form holes in our hearts—can
launch us toward sexual sin. Think about it. Because of our
brains' hardwiring, we're already handicapped regarding relationships in the first place, partly because our brains' hemi-
spheres don't talk to each other very well. Then, since our
verbal skills are rooted in the left hemisphere and our emotions are rooted in the right hemisphere, we can't easily access
our emotions verbally. That explains why it's hard to articu-
late what we're feeling. We just know we don't fit in any-
where, and we aren't connecting with anyone intimately.

Here's where our hardwiring sets us up to fall. My dad
wounded me deeply and left me lonely and aching. Do you
remember the primary way guys give and receive intimacy?
That's right, through the acts just prior to and during inter-
course. What can give guys that feeling of intimacy, that feeling of love and acceptance? Right again—the always smiling,
always available and unclothed girls of cyberspace who never
reject you and who always offer you everything they've got
while asking for nothing in return.

Without that connection with our fathers and that
acceptance as men, we are practically guaranteed to fall into
sexual sin during our teen years. Orgasmic relief is the medi-
cation for our pain. And once this becomes our crutch in our
crippled interpersonal lives, we'll drag that crutch right into
marriage. Wives often think their husbands used porn before
marriage merely to release a little sexual pressure from time

to time, so they expect the habit to vanish once the honey-
moon begins. But I'm not talking sexual pressure; I am
describing emotional wounds that run deep. If your husband
still doubts his masculinity, then his porn habit won't disap-
pear overnight no matter what you do for him sexually. 📖

1. What do you know about your husband's story? How was his relationship with his father? Do you sense that there may be some wounds
   there?

2. If your husband is willing to talk through his history, how can you
   support him? As he works on healing those wounds, his need to medi-
   cate the pain will lessen. You can't force him to talk about it, but if he
   is willing, what can you do to help?

3. Maybe you've never thought about your husband's sin from this perspective. But as you do, can you bring his wounds to God's feet? Write
   down a prayer in the following space. What would you like to ask
   God to do with your husband's pain?

If your husband isn't willing to talk through his story, that's not your responsibility. You can love and support and pray for him, but you can't carry the load of healing his hurts. If anything, just knowing that he has been wounded might help you in your understanding. Beyond that, he has to take the steps himself toward healing.

As wound after wound leaves holes in a young man's heart, he learns that intimacy is painful. He wants it, he wants to be close to someone, but no one will have him—and it hurts. He's rejected by his dad, his school buddies, and by girls. He turns to porn because it eases the pain, even if it's just for a moment.

📖 If you ask wives to explain porn's potent draw, they'll cite the sex appeal of limitless free and frisky women to the male eyes and mind. But there are more complex factors at work here. Porn provides instant soothing to emotional stress, and the easy access to Internet porn makes it difficult to wean men away from their emotional dependence on it.

Tanner said, "Sure, I've learned that sex does not fill the emptiness like I thought it would. But online porn offers the 'gentle stroking' that we males need. I can tell you this: it's better than nothing."

The trouble with this tack is that masturbation is an implosion of sexual pleasure that focuses a guy further and further into himself. Since the genuine need for interpersonal intimacy cannot be met by self-seeking sexual activity, the hunger for genuine intimacy is never fulfilled. But a "better than nothing" attitude sends him right back to the computer for that gentle stroking, which drives him further within himself, which leaves him feeling emptier still…and so it goes. 📖

📖 Have you ever noticed that you feel more lonely and isolated after watching television alone? That's because there was no human contact. Masturbation is similar. There was no real sexual encounter. Sure, the act feels sexual and the resulting climax feels like intimacy, but it actually leaves a guy feeling more alone and more ashamed than when he woke up that morning. 📖

4. Have you ever watched television to ease your loneliness? When it only helped for the moment, did that stop you from going back to it? Have you ever watched television because it was easier to do that than take the time to build friendships and intimacy? When looking at it from this perspective, is it easier to understand what might be happening with your husband? Explain.

People within the church are often hesitant to take a stance or to even discuss male sexuality. In an effort to be sensitive to young men struggling with masturbation, they either don't bring it up or they make light of it. While they may be driven by good intentions, their silence leaves young men to wonder if there is any escape from the sin that is eating them up inside. Read this young man's story from part 3 of *Every Heart Restored:*

📖 I was eleven when I first masturbated. It just kind of happened while watching a strip scene in a TV movie. For about two, three years, I didn't even know it was masturbation. It just felt good. Then in middle school, my Sunday-school teacher separated the genders for some "adolescent teaching."

Fortunately, I was taught a lot about puberty and lust. Unfortunately, my teacher was not too clear on masturbation and took a very neutral standpoint so as not to offend anyone by saying that masturbation was wrong. I took that as a green light, and from there it started to become a daily habit. But a funny thing happened. Though no one had spoken against it, I started to feel guilty about the practice. I guess that even though my Sunday-school teacher didn't make it clear, my Teacher inside me did! But by then I was hooked, and I was locked into masturbation for years. 📖

📖 You already know that our male hardwiring is prone to addictive lusts of the eyes. Now you can see how our own churches wound us with their desire to be "relevant," promoting and approving the very things that rev a guy's sexual engine into the red zone. Once there, however, masturbation eats our spirituality alive. 📖

5. If masturbation was never addressed within the confines of the church, never discussed at home, how is a boy to understand how God calls him to live sexually? Do you know what kind of teaching your husband received? Did he receive any at all? How does this help you understand him?

⬿ EVERY WOMAN'S WALK
(Your Guide to Personal Application)

In many ways your husband is floundering in a world where he has had very little guidance. Visual stimulation is affirmed at every turn, initiating and enjoying cheap sexuality is espoused as "manhood" on most television shows, and the church has remained largely silent. Even to confess sexual sin and addictive drives is extremely difficult, and most men find themselves too ashamed to do so.

So the Enemy uses that shame, their fear, and our sense of betrayal, and sabotages marriages left and right.

What can you do? How can you stop this from happening in your own marriage? Your first step is to remain closely connected to your First Love. This is huge. Even as you understand and try to stand by your husband, you will need to dip frequently into the well of love God has for you. You are fully immersed in a difficult situation. You are struggling with your own hurts and frustrations, and you are now being asked to understand those of your husband. Without Christ, this is nearly impossible. But with Him, you can extend grace when you don't feel it, extend love when you are hurting, and extend compassion when you need the same for yourself. And that kind of response stops the Enemy dead in his tracks—giving you and your relationship a true shot at restoration.

6. As you have walked through some of the potential motives for your husband's sin, you may be feeling overwhelmed, wondering how this will all work out. Remember the truth that we continue to stand on—your God is bigger than any of this. He is able to sustain and comfort you, giving you strength when you need it most. Take a minute and write down as a prayer to Him exactly what you are feeling. Let Him meet you at your point of need.

7. Now that you have set your heart before God, write what you have learned in the last two chapters about the potential motives behind your husband's sin. Did anything in particular sound like his experience? What have you learned?

8. If your husband is willing to work through some of these wounds, there is true hope for your relationship. Can you begin to see it? Explain.

9. If your husband is unwilling, begin to pray that his heart might be softened. Write your request here.

👥 EVERY WOMAN'S TALK

(Going Deeper—Constructive Topics and Questions for Group Discussion)

(For the twelve-week track, save these questions for week nine.)

📖 These broken relationships cause great internal anguish and insecurity in the sons, leaving them to seek intimacy wherever they can find it.

Sexual sin flourishes in the wake of bad or broken family relationships. The splintering effects of divorce or parental death shatter our worlds. Teens, rather than feeling accepted and cherished by their parents, feel as though they've been cast aside. They spend their lives searching for love and meaning, when it should have been provided in the home by a loving mother and a loving father.

But even when a father sticks around, the wounds inflicted can lead to deep bondage. 📖

A. Does this quote, combined with the information provided in the last two chapters, help in your understanding of your husband's struggle? Explain.

B. How does your understanding translate into action? What can you do to convey your support? Share it with the group and ask for accountability and prayer.

loving the man you married

Eight-week track—Week Six

Twelve-week track—Week Eight

Janice had big dreams about her future. As a little girl she consumed "happily ever after" tales and fantasized about the day her knight in shining armor would arrive. She had it all planned out. They would meet, marry, have three children, one cat, and two dogs. Her husband would love her with an undying love, and they would spend their sunset years traveling and savoring the best life had to offer.

Oh, she knew it would be tough. They'd have their hiccups along the way. But God meant for her to live happily ever after, right? He meant for her to marry the perfect man of her dreams, didn't He?

Janice did marry, and unfortunately her dreams began to fade as the reality of careers, bills, and housekeeping came crashing in. Not only that, but her husband didn't seem very interested in her sexually. She'd waited until the wedding day, and his lack of attention now left her wondering if she was somehow deficient. She grew angry. Angry with her husband and angry with God. Finally, when her husband confessed that he struggled with pornography, she was ready to throw in the towel.

This was not what she had expected out of marriage, and she began to wonder if she had made a mistake.

📖 EVERY WOMAN'S TRUTH
(Your Personal Journey into God's Word)

Facing the loss of a childhood dream can be devastating. This is true for many women—even in a *good* marriage scenario. Nothing can live up to the expectation we often place on married life. We are taught as young girls that our prince will come and make everything wonderful. Through story after story, we are told that life doesn't really begin until the man of our dreams comes to rescue us. When he does, he will make us happy, he will adore us, he will make life what it was always meant to be.

Even without pornography entering the picture, women fight the sadness of broken expectations and dreams after the wedding day. Enter sexual wanderings, and you might as well rip the rug out from underneath us.

In this place of disillusionment it becomes tempting to believe that we have made a mistake, that we should do something different, that God must have had something else planned. But that might not be the truth—and even if it were, God honors marriage and asks us to fight for it. He is the One who can take broken pieces and fashion something beautiful. He is the One who sees things we don't see. He is the One who exposes our weaknesses so He can build strength. He cares about much more than our immediate happiness.

> He is the Rock, his works are perfect,
> and all his ways are just.
> A faithful God who does no wrong,
> upright and just is he. (Deuteronomy 32:4)

"For my thoughts are not your thoughts,

 neither are your ways my ways," declares the LORD.

"As the heavens are higher than the earth,

 so are my ways higher than your ways

 and my thoughts than your thoughts." (Isaiah 55:8-9)

This is the word that came to Jeremiah from the LORD: "Go down to the potter's house, and there I will give you my message." So I went down to the potter's house, and I saw him working at the wheel. But the pot he was shaping from the clay was marred in his hands; so the potter formed it into another pot, shaping it as seemed best to him.

Then the word of the LORD came to me: "O house of Israel, can I not do with you as this potter does?" declares the LORD. "Like clay in the hand of the potter, so are you in my hand, O house of Israel." (Jeremiah 18:1-6)

And we know that in all things God works for the good of those who love him, who have been called according to his purpose. (Romans 8:28)

We don't always know what God is up to in our lives. In a perfect world, we would be able to physically walk with Him, talk with Him, and know His thoughts. But in a broken world, we have to trust Him even when we don't understand. First, know this: it's not His will that your husband's sin would wound and damage you. He hates what perversity does to marriage, and He grieves with you over the sadness. But it *may* be His will that your husband's sin be exposed, that the hurts underneath be addressed and healed, and that in the process your own weaknesses and wounds be healed as well.

Look again at Jeremiah 18:4: "The pot he was shaping was marred." The pot was marred, so he was reshaping it into a new pot. He was taking what was broken and creating something new. The reshaping process couldn't have been pleasant for that little pot; he may have thought he was being destroyed. But no, the master knew what he was doing. As the promise reads in Deuteronomy 32:4, "A faithful God who does no wrong, upright and just is he."

1. Do you trust that even though things have not turned out as expected, God could still fashion your marriage into something beautiful? Why?

2. Meditate on the scriptures listed. What do they say about His ways and His character? We may not know the why or how, but is our God trustworthy? Explain.

3. Take the next few lines and talk to God about this reshaping process. Call out to Him the things that are in your heart—your longings and your fears. He is ready and willing to hear them all.

☑ EVERY WOMAN'S CHOICE

(Questions for Personal Reflection and Examination)

📖 Providing a lifetime soul mate *is* on God's list, but how soon we'll *seem* like soul mates on a day-to-day basis depends upon the softness of our hearts to His sanctification work, both inside and outside the bedroom. That's part of God's higher ways.

He wants happiness for you, but He *also* wants what is best for you *and* what is best for your husband. He knows that this sexual disaster in your marriage will force you to learn how to love the unlovely, the very bedrock trait of Christian character, and He knows that what's happened will shatter your husband's defenses so that the Lord can move in closer and begin healing his long-festering wounds. 📖

📖 I know what you're thinking: *If it is, then I've been duped. I didn't sign up for this.* Maybe so. But all too often we ignore God's higher-ways point of view and miss His vision for our marriages, which He's intended as our very own under-the-radar, no-headline, home mission field. Perhaps you've spent years asking God to reveal His will for your life, when all along He's been asking in return, *How are you doing with that little part of My will that I've already revealed to you regarding your marriage?*

Emily wrote, "I feel like God has fed me to the wolves in this marriage. I feel like I was conned into what you call a mission field."

We're easily thrown off by our husbands' filth, aren't we? We resent having married into this dark, sexual underside of humanity. 📖

📖 What about you? There's no question that you are your husband's wife. But when you look in that mirror of your heart, what do you see? Are you also your husband's sister? If you're to handle his wounds well on Christ's behalf, you'll have to act like a loving sister, too.

Christ's example is clear. Jesus was wounded plenty, just like you—it happens to all of us. But while it's okay to *be* wounded, it's not okay to *stay* wounded. 📖

4. As much as it may frustrate you that your marriage has not turned out as planned, can you see God working in the midst of this situation? How is He changing your husband? How is He changing you?

5. When you think of your husband and your home as a potential mission field, does that strengthen your resolve to love him through this? Why or why not?

6. If you are having some trouble moving past your wounds to the point of facing his, what can you do to take some additional steps toward healing?

~ EVERY WOMAN'S WALK
(Your Guide to Personal Application)

Here's where things can get difficult. Each situation is unique, each marriage is unique, and each person is unique. For one woman, loving her husband might mean a separation—especially if he is doing nothing to deal with his sin. For another woman, loving her husband might mean pulling him close and granting him grace. And for another woman, it will be about holding him accountable and being his friend.

As a wife wanting to do the right thing, which course should you take?

As Brenda shared about her journey with Fred, it began with her. She first made herself accountable for her own attitudes and actions. She determined that she would do her best to respond like Christ would. Did she always succeed? No. But she did what she could to monitor her own behavior first. And then she loved her husband as the situation called for it, being a helpmate, a lover, or a friend—always staying close to her heavenly Father so that He could sustain and help her.

As Fred shares toward the end of chapter 17, "I asked her about her approach one time, and she said, 'My reactions to you are always a choice, and when I can't love you for your sake because you are being so harsh, I can always find a way to love you for Jesus' sake because of what He's done for me.'"

Again, was Brenda perfect? No. Did she get angry and lash out and sometimes make the wrong choice? Yes, just like all of us. But she remained consistent in going to Christ for His strength and for a reminder of what His love meant to her so that she could willingly pass it on.

7. When you read about the different paths to take, what do you think would best help your husband at this stage? Is he willing to seek help? Can you be his lover and his friend in that process? Or is he unrepentant and stuck in his sin? In that case, can you find the courage to step away and separate from him—allowing him to feel the consequences of his choice? Describe your situation and how you can best love him.

8. What are some practical ways that you can find strength and comfort in the midst of this? You will need time with God in order to see clearly. How can you make that happen?

9. Take a moment and write down the things that drew you to your husband. In the middle of this chaos, as you do what you can to stand

with him, your heart might need some reminders. What do you or what have you loved about him?

🙂🙂 EVERY WOMAN'S TALK

(Going Deeper—Constructive Topics and Questions for Group Discussion)

(For the twelve-week track, save these questions for week nine.)

> 📖 You need that broader view too. Sure, his sin is betraying and crushing you, but it is also revealing his deeper wounds and addictions below the surface. He's not just a straying husband but a brother lost in the futility of his thinking and now corrupted by his deceitful desires. It's not just about you.
>
> The way I came to view things, I was not just Fred's wife, called to respectfully submit to his leadership and to always be ravished in his arms. I was *also* his good Samaritan, compelled by my love to dress his wounds, and *also* his friend, taking on the "iron sharpens iron" role described in Proverbs 27:17. 📖

A. What have you learned from this chapter? What practical truth can you apply to your situation?

B. As a group you have gathered together for a number of weeks now. Ask your group how they perceive your situation. Sometimes another set of godly eyes can give us the perspective we need. How would they suggest you love your husband in this particular season? Good Samaritan? Accountability partner? Lover? Keep in mind you should always bring the counsel you receive to God's feet and ask for clarification, but the input of others can be valuable in helping you to discern your next steps.

C. When you think of loving your husband through this, it might bring up a sense of resentment, fear, or anger. Tell the group of your feelings and ask for their prayers. You are not in this alone.

rebuilding trust

For the twelve-week track, complete discussion questions for weeks seven and eight this week.

Eight-week track—Week Seven
Twelve-week track—Week Ten

Lanna felt good about the progress she and Matt had made. It was six months since her husband had looked at anything pornographic. He had solid accountability in his life, and he seemed to be growing. She, too, had grown in the process. She now understood that she'd been too dependent on him for her happiness. He'd been her entire world. Since discovering his struggle with pornography, she'd cultivated some healthy friendships and her relationship with God was deeper than before.

But Lanna was still afraid. Matt had relapsed twice, and every day she battled the fear that he would relapse again. What would she do if he failed to win this battle? She didn't know if she could handle another slip down that path. It took too much out of her. She had a hard time trusting Matt, even though she wanted to believe he was putting this behind him.

Lanna wondered how long it would be before she would feel normal again—whatever "normal" might be.

📖 EVERY WOMAN'S TRUTH

(Your Personal Journey into God's Word)

If you are dealing with pornography or sexual addiction in your marriage, you already know what it means to lose faith in your husband. Your trust has been damaged, and you're afraid to trust again.

It takes time to rebuild trust. Time, and evidence of change. You are not obligated to trust him as soon as he takes a step forward. It is only with time that he can earn back what he destroyed. As he works to earn your trust, over time you will be able to open your heart to him—but this is a gradual process. and that's okay.

> 📖 Trust can only exist in relationship. Oh, I can hope against hope that Fred'll keep his word, and I can certainly play mind games with myself like Charlie Brown does with Lucy, but real trust can only come when I have full confidence in Fred's faithfulness. Only one thing can bring that confidence—his consistent, faithful actions. My love, forgiveness, and commitment may require nothing of Fred, but my trust requires plenty. Without right actions, he can't have my trust, and if he wants my trust, it's all on him.
>
> Husbands often hate this responsibility, but you needn't apologize for it. And you needn't feel guilty if your husband sneers, "If you loved me, you would trust me."
>
> Baloney. Trust and love are two different things. 📖

Do these ideas offer you some relief? Building trust takes time!

But you may be wondering, *What do I do in the meantime? I can't stay in this place of mistrust and try to be married!*

Here is the truth: maybe you can't trust your husband yet, but you can trust God. He is big enough, strong enough, and faithful enough to take care of you and your marriage as you cling to Him.

Listen to this:

> The LORD himself goes before you and will be with you; he
> will never leave you nor forsake you. Do not be afraid; do
> not be discouraged. (Deuteronomy 31:8)

> Those who know your name will trust in you,
>> for you, LORD, have never forsaken those who seek you.
>>> (Psalm 9:10)

> When I am afraid,
>> I will trust in you. (Psalm 56:3)

> Trust in the LORD with all your heart
>> and lean not on your own understanding;
> in all your ways acknowledge him,
>> and he will make your paths straight. (Proverbs 3:5-6)

> Who of you by worrying can add a single hour to his life?
> (Luke 12:25)

> Do not let your hearts be troubled. Trust in God; trust also
> in me. (John 14:1)

God is trustworthy. Even when everything and everyone else is not, even when you are afraid or nervous about what might be coming, He is there, and He is *still* trustworthy. It's very easy to get caught up wondering what your husband might be up to; it's even easier to play scenarios in your mind: *What if he* _____*? Well, if he does, then I'm going to*

_____*.*

We can spend hours worrying and plotting how to protect ourselves. That is not to say that our worry isn't founded or that our concerns aren't valid. But you don't have to stay in that place! No matter what comes, God is with you. He is with your husband. And He will sustain you, no matter what the circumstance.

1. If your husband has been "sober" for some time, do you worry about a relapse? If he's right in the middle of his struggle, do you wonder if he will ever win? What are your fears right now?

2. Look at the truth of God's character from His Word. What do the previously quoted scriptures say about God? What does that mean for your fears and worries?

3. How can you consciously set your concerns before Him? Take a moment and write a prayer in the space below. Pour out all your thoughts and remind yourself of His character. While your husband may be working on rebuilding trust with you, your God is trustworthy right now! Tell Him how you feel:

☑ **EVERY WOMAN'S CHOICE**
(Questions for Personal Reflection and Examination)

📖 In short, it is self-defeating to work first upon your trust in your husband. It is not uncommon for a wife to focus on her husband's behavior, looking earnestly for anything from him that demonstrates that she should trust him again. She watches every move intently, and more often than not, the husband fails under that pressure.

It's far wiser to work on your husband's trustworthiness to God by defending God's boundaries in your marriage and exposing your husband's well-crafted image to the light. Not only does that take the pressure off of everyone, but it is also the proper target....

This is ultimately between your husband and the King. You needn't jump him every time he blows it. Trust God. When you aren't speaking, you can be certain that God is. 📖

📖 If he's truly repented, trustworthy acts will become second nature to him. You have every right to play a role in defining what trustworthiness means to you, and you can expect him to come through for you. 📖

4. Do you trust your husband now? Explain.

5. If you don't trust your husband, and perhaps you are constantly fearful, how does that affect your daily life?

6. Knowing that God "has your back" and is able to speak to your husband, does that make you feel more secure? Why or why not?

7. As you read the sections from these wives who have been through very similar circumstances, what can you learn from their reactions?

⟪ EVERY WOMAN'S WALK
(Your Guide to Personal Application)

It seems easy to say, "Trust God, and all will be well." There are situations where such solid truth only comes across as a tired cliché. *How do I trust God? What does that look like?* When you're waking up in the middle of the night, when your thoughts are consumed during the day, how do you simply stop and trust God?

You don't simply stop. That wouldn't be realistic or even possible (unless you are a spiritual guru of some sort). What *is* possible is to take your hurts to God. Every time worries come to mind, call out to God. *God, it's me again. It's five minutes later. You told me I could trust You. You told me You were enough. Well, I'm here again. I'm mad, I'm afraid, and I need You.*

If it's ten times a day or fifty times a day, His ear is bent to your cry. He will be there. He is faithful. And what you will find is that over time you won't worry as much, you won't be as afraid. You will find peace.

The best thing? As you feel peace in trusting God, you will be better able to extend trust to your husband. You will be stronger, less vulnerable to the what ifs, because even if he does let you down (and he will), God is big enough and strong enough to hold you both.

Another thought? When you are anxious and nothing seems to comfort you, He may be trying to tell *you* something. Perhaps there's a hurt in your own heart that He wants to heal. Maybe your discomfort will cause you to finally bring it all to the Grand Physician, the Good Surgeon, the One who is able to find what is broken and heal it.

How do you know which scenario it is? You stay close to Him, and you stay close to godly friends and counsel. You pray and journal. This is not a time to fill up your schedule and stay busy; this is a time to strategically invest your time with the only One who can take away your fear and rebuild your trust.

Does this have anything to do with your husband? Yes. Absolutely. As he makes better choices, as he seeks God, it will be possible to trust him again. But please hear this: unless you trust God, the moment your husband lets you down again, you will be hurt in ways that can damage you. But if you trust God's goodness, God's hand on your husband's life, and God's love for you—then no matter what comes, you may hurt, but you will be safe.

8. What is one practical step you can take in trusting God? How can you facilitate that trust? What practice can you incorporate into your life to help you lean on Him?

9. How does trusting God with your husband help you, your husband, and your marriage—no matter what the scenario?

👩👩 Every Woman's Talk

(Going Deeper—Constructive Topics and Questions for Group Discussion)

(For the twelve-week track, save these questions for week twelve.)

Mary would hear his words of repentance but see no actions. John dismissed her feelings with a callous attitude: "I asked God for forgiveness. He forgave me, so let's move on. What's your problem?" And as for his actions, John's attitude was, "It's a guy thing. It's wrong, but hey, we're guys. Don't be so legalistic."

This made Mary question who he was spiritually. She felt betrayed; he married her without telling her about this problem. Had she known, she'd have run from the altar, and he knew that too.

> 📖 He should be telling you about the action steps he is
> taking, and he should be asking you for ways that he can build
> your trust. Katie had this to say about her husband's steps:
>
> "One of the primary things he did was to write me a con-
> tract, and the best part was that this was his idea. He com-
> mitted to join an accountability group, began investing in
> marriage-builder books and tapes, and learned some steps he
> could take to stay pure while traveling out of town. Really,
> the list goes on. I'm pretty proud of him. He has kept his
> promises—other than a few delays in finishing some of the
> books he's promised to read. I think it came to a point where
> he realized this trap could cost him everything he loves, and
> it just wasn't worth it." 📖

Here are two different men with two completely different reactions to their sin. One is callous and harsh, the other is working hard to set things right. God is equally trustworthy in both situations. For a wife of an unrepentant man stuck in the middle of sin, there are options. She has every right to stand for God's boundaries in marriage, to hold her husband accountable, to refuse to accept his behavior. God will stand with her. As she leans on His faithfulness, He will equip her to be bold when she needs to be bold and to be tender when it's called for. For the second wife, God is also trustworthy. He will help her as she learns to trust again, as she overcomes fear and rebuilds intimacy. He is the author of new beginnings.

A. In the spectrum of completely unrepentant to fully accountable, where is your husband now? Share with the group.

B. What do you need from God right now? Do you believe He is trustworthy? Why or why not?

C. What have you learned in this chapter that you can apply to your current situation? Share with the group what you have decided and ask for their prayers and accountability.

drawing on hope

Eight-week track—Week Eight
Twelve-week track—Week Eleven

Danielle lay beside her husband. His arms were wrapped around her, and she was tucked into the warmth of his body. She'd never felt so safe in his embrace. They'd gone through such a roller coaster of emotion after he shared his struggles with pornography. Married for nine years, Danielle had learned of his betrayal only two years into their marriage. He'd been viewing pornography since he was a teenager, and his addiction had only worsened with time.

But he'd faced up to the struggle. He found accountability, and he read insightful and challenging books. Still, it was painful. He went back five different times before finally letting it go for good. Over the last few years he had earned her trust by staying accountable, growing spiritually, and inviting her to question him whenever she needed to ask.

Their relationship was sweeter than it had ever been before. Both of them had gone through counseling, together and individually. They'd both looked at their own hearts and kept an eye on their actions and reactions. They'd called to and been dependent on God. Slowly, trust had been earned and rebuilt.

For the first time, Danielle was grateful for the journey. If they'd never gone through it, they may never have reached the level of intimacy they now shared. She knew it could have gone either way—they both had a choice to stay stuck or to move forward. Thankfully, step by faltering step, they had moved forward.

And as she tucked in closer, feeling the beating of his heart through his warm skin, she had to smile. This was what marriage was meant to be. After nine hard years, she was truly enjoying her husband's touch and presence. She smiled toward the ceiling and thanked her heavenly Father. He was indeed a God of restoration and relationship. And Danielle was beyond grateful.

EVERY WOMAN'S TRUTH
(Your Personal Journey into God's Word)

Depending on where you are in your personal journey, you might read the preceding story with skepticism. *Right,* you might think to yourself, *like that's going to happen to me. My situation is totally different!*

Your situation might be different, but your God is the same. Restoration is possible! Brenda and Fred shared their own path with you in the book. Their marriage is strong, their love for each other sincere. Others have known success; they have seen the light at the end of the tunnel.

So what made it work?

In each of their journeys, there were common threads. Both Fred and Brenda were trying to make it work, both were willing to take responsibility for their actions, and both wanted to pursue Christ.

Yet if you don't share those ingredients, don't give up hope! Pursue counseling, invite some prayer warriors to come alongside you, stand firm, monitor your own heart, hold your husband accountable for his actions, and call out faithfully to your God. He will not abandon or forsake you.

Either way, God has a hope for your marriage. He has a future in mind for your love. Listen to what He has to say:

> For this reason a man will leave his father and mother and
> be united to his wife, and they will become *one flesh*.
> (Genesis 2:24)

> May your fountain be blessed,
>   and may you rejoice in the wife of your youth.
> A loving doe, a graceful deer—
>   may her breasts satisfy you always,
>   may you ever be captivated by her love. (Proverbs 5:18-19)

> Enjoy life with your wife, whom you love. (Ecclesiastes 9:9)

Or like these verses condensed from Song of Songs:

Husband:
You have stolen my heart, my sister, my bride;
    you have stolen my heart
with one glance of your eyes....

How delightful is your love, my sister, my bride!...

Your head crowns you like Mount Carmel.
    Your hair is like royal tapestry;
    the king is held captive by its tresses.
How beautiful you are and how pleasing,
    O love, with your delights!
        (Song of Songs 4:9-10; 7:5-6)

Wife:

My [husband] is radiant and ruddy,
    outstanding among ten thousand.
His head is purest gold;
        his hair is wavy
        and black as a raven....

His mouth is sweetness itself;
        he is altogether lovely.
This is my lover, this is my friend....

I belong to my lover,
        and his desire is for me....

Let us go early to the vineyards...
        there I will give you my love.
The mandrakes send out their fragrance,
        and at our door is every delicacy,
both new and old,
        that I have stored up for you, my lover.
            (Song of Songs 5:10-11,16; 7:10,12-13)

1. When you read the previously quoted scriptures, what thoughts go through your mind?

2. Do you believe that God has hope, life, and passion for your marriage? Why or why not?

3. Take a moment and prepare a prayer for your marriage and your sexual intimacy, a prayer that puts words to the dreams you have. Use God's picture of what marriage should look like and craft the prayer according to your current situation. If you are just a few steps from real intimacy, put that before God. If it feels like an impossible dream, write that to Him as well. He wants to know and hear your heart!

☑ EVERY WOMAN'S CHOICE

(Questions for Personal Reflection and Examination)

Your complete trust in God can be the very thing that jars your husband to his senses, as Debbie found out recently:

> 📖 After my husband's affair, God really ministered to me. He had me study the life of David and encouraged me to believe that although my husband struggled with sexual sins, he could still be a man after God's heart.
>
> Maybe that is why the second incident a few years later rocked me as much as it did. I felt like I had *already* paid the

ultimate price to save our marriage, and yet here we go again. I cannot say that mercy rose up in me this time! Although it may have sounded like a harsh threat when I told my husband I was leaving, my fearless confidence in God and in His ability to take care of me shook my husband to his toes.

For the first time, I think Jay realized that marriage was something fragile, and he could lose everything he loved by participating in sexual trysts and downloading a bunch of stupid pictures. This time he found someone who could counsel him on this struggle—a godly accountability partner.

There was something different and lasting now. I guess you could say he was ready to grow up, take the hard steps, and make the hard choices to open his life up to others and to humble himself before God. Oddly enough, our sex life quickly became better than ever. For the first time in a long time, I felt like he really knew I was there in bed with him. Maybe there was more of a reason to invest in my pleasure since the other wells had run dry, but who really cares? All I knew is that I liked his efforts. 📖

Brenda shared something similar in chapter 20:

📖 My confidence in Fred's spiritual protection is unbounded. I never wonder if there are open cracks in our spiritual defenses where the Enemy can slip into our lives. Christianity is not a game to Fred, and image means nothing. He'd rather *be* a Christian than seem like one.

Fred has every right to make the decisions for our family because it's God's plan, but even if it weren't, he's earned that right through his actions. He's proven in battle that his commitment to the Lord and his love for his family are the highest priorities in his life, and we simply rest in his strength.

This normal, godly pattern leaves everyone flourishing, and this wouldn't be possible if blatant sin were clogging things up. I know who Fred is, and in the secret places of life, I know where he will not go.

Let's freeze that frame for a moment. What I'm describing should be normal family life, and every wife deserves a shot at normalcy. I sure didn't start at normal in my marriage, and heaven knows that most of us don't. But with our help and Christ's grace, our marriages can get there. It won't happen over a long weekend, but this is what you deserve, this is what God has promised you, and in the long run, this is what God calls your husband to deliver. 📖

4. In the first story, Debbie held her husband accountable by letting him feel the consequences for his actions. He chose to betray the marriage again, and she put her foot down. She would not let him continue to damage her heart. He turned things around, made different choices, sought accountability. In the second story, Brenda talks of Fred's choices as well—his willingness to lead spiritually, his prayer life, and so on. In both stories, the relationship has been restored. What does that tell you about God's ability to build relationship, no matter what the circumstance? Explain what that means for you and your marriage.

5. Where is your marriage? Are you still raw and bleeding, or are you drawing closer to real hope? If you could look down the road five years (through God's eyes), what might you see? Explain.

⌒ EVERY WOMAN'S WALK
(Your Guide to Personal Application)

It would be wonderful if every woman reading this book would experience a happy ending. It would be ideal if every marriage was restored, every husband was repentant and teachable, and every woman forgiving and blessed continuously with hope.

That's not realistic. You may be reading these words in the middle of a war zone, and it's not going to get any better. You've tried everything from prayer to counseling to putting your foot down. Your husband has resisted you at every turn. It may feel as if your marriage might be over. Like we've said at several turns, if this describes you, find a support network. Draw close to your God. Lean on friends. God can still do an amazing work in your life, even if your marriage has reached an end. He can take the broken pieces of your heart and bring hope and joy and peace. Walk with your head held high. You are a beautiful woman, and your God is absolutely crazy about you. It's okay. With godly counsel, you can move on.

But if your situation is not so bleak, there is hope. You've seen your husband move forward, grieve his actions, and desire to do better. Your next step is to cling tightly to your God, draw your strength from Him, stand by your husband, and hope. Hope that your relationship can be sweet, remember what you have loved about him, and imagine what it will be like to be safe in his arms again.

This is not an easy road. Keep in mind that it may get worse before it gets better. Your anger may blindside you in a bad moment and his sin might blindside him as well. But your God is bigger. Bigger than the hurt, bigger than the sin, bigger than the betrayal. He is ready, willing, and able to restore your marriage beyond your expectation.

6. Knowing your marriage and knowing God, what is your next step? Be specific.

Every Woman's Talk

(Going Deeper—Constructive Topics and Questions for Group Discussion)

(For the twelve-week track, save these questions for week twelve, but do complete discussion questions for weeks ten *and* eleven this week.)

As a group you have walked through weeks of discovery together. You have learned about the validity of the betrayal you experienced, the shame, the beauty that remains in you. You've learned about your husband's choices, what may lie behind them, and how he is wired. You've learned about trusting again, that it's a process that takes time. Most important, you've learned that God is absolutely with you every step of the way. He is not a distant, disengaged God; He is fully involved in your life and eager to be there for you. As you trust His character and draw closer to His heart, you will be able to stand firm no matter what comes.

A. Over the last few weeks together, what have you learned that will help you in your marriage today?

B. What practical steps have you incorporated over the last few weeks? Have they helped you? Why or why not? Share your discoveries with the group so you can continue to learn from each other.

C. In the space below, write down specific requests for the people in your group. Write down names and what you can pray for them. Ask them to do the same for you. If the group agrees, do your best to touch base periodically. Hold one another up on this journey toward healing. God put you together for a unique purpose; you may need each other beyond this environment. Be open to that.

don't keep it to yourself

Congratulations on finishing this workbook! We pray you have found encouragement for your heart and soul as well as hope and healing for your marriage. We pray that you now have a clear understanding of your husband's battle for sexual purity and fresh insight into your role as his helpmate. But most of all, we pray that your call in this storm is clear and that your commitment to Him is sure.

If you've just completed the *Every Heart Restored Workbook* on your own and benefited from it, why not invite a group of other women to experience similar hope and healing? This will not only keep you accountable but will also enable you to assist other women caught in the same battle. When women encourage one another to open up about their struggles in this area, they find so much of the support and help they seek.

You'll find more information about starting such a group on pages 2 and 3 in the section titled "Questions You May Have About This Workbook."